MEMORIES OF MY JAMAICAN
mother

Doreen Patricia Reid

© 2007 Doreen Patricia Ried
First Edition
10 9 8 7 6 5 4 3 2 1

All rights reserved. No part of this book may be reproduced, stored in a retrieval system, or transmitted, in any form or by any means, electronic, mechanical, photocopying, recording, or otherwise, without the prior written permission of the publishers or author.

If you have bought this book without a cover you should be aware that it is "stolen" property. The publishers and author have not received any payment for the "stripped" book, if it is printed without their authorization.

All LMH titles, imprints and distributed lines are available at special quantity discounts for bulk purchases for sales promotion, premiums, fund-raising, educational or institutional use.

Edited by Nicola Brown/K. Sean Harris
Cover Design by Sanya Dockery
Book Design, Layout & Typesetting by Sanya Dockery

Published by: LMH Publishing Limited
7 Norman Road,
LOJ Industrial Complex
Building 10
Kingston C.S.O., Jamaica
Tel: 876-938-0005; 938-0712
Fax: 876-759-8752
Email: lmhbookpublishing@cwjamaica.com
Website: www.lmhpublishing.com

Printed in U. S. A.   ISBN: 978-976-8202-44-4

DEDICATION

This book is dedicated to her husband, Lennie Reid, and her eight children, other family members, friends and well wishers.

ACKNOWLEDGEMENT

The author of the book, Ms. Doreen Reid, would like to thank the following persons for their invaluable contribution to the publication of this book:

- Ms. Marcikie Henry
- Ms. Kadian Douglas
- Ms. Prudence Hines
- Ms. Sheryl Williamson
- Ms. Conchita Lebert

FOREWORD

I did not have the privilege of knowing Phyllis Reid. But, on seeing her broad smile and the way she sits proudly upright in her picture on the cover of this book, I can agree with her daughter that she was "a strong and beautiful black Jamaican woman" the kind of person that I think of as an old-time Jamaican mother who espoused positive family values; who loved and represented her husband and children; who cared about and for her family, and for whom 'family' meant all those with whom she came in contact on a daily basis.

Knowing her daughter, Doreen, the author of this book, also attests to the kind of person she must have been; someone who knew poverty and adversity but whom through it all, magnified her creator, thanking Him always for her life and for what she had; someone whom although suffering personal disappointment time and again always had a smile, a friendly word and a willingness to "tun her han mek fashion".

This is the kind of woman Phyllis Reid must have been. This is the kind of woman I see in her daughter, Doreen, who she so lovingly reared. I pay tribute to Phyllis Reid in death. I pay tribute to her daughter and pray for her continued success in life.

I encourage you to read, enjoy and reflect upon the words she has written. They will surely help you to strive to be a better person.

Vilma McClenan
BSc. (UWI 1965), Dip. Ed. (UWI 1969), MA. (Univ. of London 1998)
Academic Programme Coordinator at UWI Distance Education Centre, UWI, Mona Campus

MEMORIES OF MY JAMAICAN MOTHER

The purpose of writing this book is to honour my mom, Phyliss Blake-Reid, and give her the same recognition as my father, Lennie Reid. They both played a very important role in my life, making me the professional I am today. This book is to help persons overcome grief by empowering their spirits and building their confidence. It will also strengthen them and give them a sense of hope, especially persons whose mothers are not among them because of death, separation or migration.

When prospective mothers read this book, it will motivate them to be better mothers in the future. It will teach them certain creative skills, which in fact, will allow them to earn a living throughout life. It is hoped that whenever this book is read it will help mothers to effectively communicate with their children.

Coping with life's tragedies is another issue that is dealt with. However, despite this, it is quite humorous as it will cause you to laugh and reflect upon the good times that you have spent with your mother. Because of this, it will help alleviate those moments when you are disheartened, thinking about the loss of your mother, and will give you the courage to move on with your life.

It is said that "a mother's duty is a well-rounded one, 24/7 around the clock. She deserves the best a child could give." It is with this adage in mind that it was necessary to instruct children how to give their mothers the love and appreciation that they deserve and not to "scatter the roses after [they're] gone". After all it's true, for when a man "can get another wife, [he] cannot get another mother."

CONTENTS

Introduction	
Life in the Country	1
From Rural to Urban	4
Mom finds Her Husband	5
A Warm Community	7
A Family Woman and Disciplinarian	9
Values and Attitudes	11
A Skilful and Talented Woman	13
Mom Overcomes the Odds	15
Mom, A Community Woman	16
A Helpful and Industrious Woman	20
Mom, A Powerful and Strong Black Woman	23
Mom Watches her Children Excel	25
A God Fearing and Devoted Mom	27
A Devout Christian	28
Retirement	30
Mom Reflects	31
Illness, Hospitalization and Death	32
Tributes	35
Lessons Learned	49

INTRODUCTION

"Everything I am or ever hope to be, I owe to my angel mother."
—*Abraham Lincoln (1809-1865)*

Humble, hardworking, selfless. My mother, Phyllis Blake Reid, is all this and much more. A devout Christian with strong family values, Mom was always there for her husband and children. She communicated well with her children and taught them that despite being visually impaired, they should be independent and strive to accomplish their goals by being ardent workers. Though Mom was a warm, loving and kind mother, being as stern as she was, she never had any qualms about applying the rod when we did something wrong. Phyllis never refused to give her family the love, support and care a mother and wife should give, and even though her husband was blind, she never used this as an opportunity to be unfaithful to him.

These exquisite attributes were not only seen by her family members as she could never refuse to help anyone no matter what the task at hand was. She was a community woman devoted to her island, Jamaica, and the well being of its citizens. Because of this, although she was a poor woman, she never hesitated to sharing the little that she had.

She always encouraged others to, "Trust in the Lord and He will come through for you," and never ceased to look to Him in her times of adversity.

INTRODUCTION

A true and faithful wife, a loving mother, a genuine Christian, a kind friend, that's my mother, Phyllis Blake Reid.

My dream and aspiration is to see a rebuilding of the family unit. This will enable our children to adopt positive family values that they will pass on to their generation in order to build a better community, country and the society at large.

Memories of our mom will never depart but will always linger in our hearts.

LIFE IN THE COUNTRY

Mrs. Phyliss Reid, otherwise called Mommy, Phyliss, Reidy and Sister Reid, was born on November 23, 1932, to Diana Brown and George Blake in the district of Newfield in Newport, Manchester. She was the second of five children, one boy who died and four girls. She grew up in a single parent home in a small white house surrounded by grass and many fruit trees. Her mother tried her best in taking care of them and ensured that they all went to school.

Mom attended the Bethabra Infant School and then moved on to the Bethabra All Age School. Because it was a poor neighbourhood, it was the norm for students to attend school barefooted and not everyone had a book. Though mom complained bitterly about having to walk in the hot, burning, sun barefooted on the asphalt, she was never tardy for school or her classes and she took great pride in her appearance. She always made sure that her feet and uniform were clean because during her school days, the students had to form a line outside the classroom in order to be inspected thoroughly by the teacher before entering the room. If the children were not attired properly they would be punished. Even the boys were prohibited from entering the classroom if their hair were not properly combed.

LIFE IN THE COUNTRY

Church was also a very important aspect of mom's life. As a child she religiously attended the Open Bible Church every Sunday morning although her mother and uncle worshipped at a Seventh Day Adventist Church. But during festive and holy seasons, my grandma and mother, along with the rest of her community, enjoyed observing most of the traditional rites associated with each season. Grandma used to rear fowls specially for Christmas time. During the Easter celebrations, on Good Friday, a broken egg was placed into a glass of water. This was done as early as possible before the sun rose. It was believed that whatever shape the egg took was indicative of one's future. For instance, a coffin symbolized death, a ship or an airplane symbolized travel and a ring was for marriage. Also, on Good Friday, a nut tree was cut at twelve noon and it was rumoured that bloody water flowed from it.

Life in the country was not equipped with all the luxuries that we now see. For one, piped water was a scarce commodity and so tanks were used to store water. Similar to that of piped water, tank water served many purposes inclusive of watering plants, giving their animals to drink and for domestic purposes. Whenever the tanks were dried, drums would be used to catch the rainfall which was then boiled and used.

In addition to not having the convenience of piped water, mom had to use thatched brooms and coconut brushes to clean. This was because the houses were built with board floors, not tiles. With the advance of technology mom often told us that we take life for granted.

Luckily, living near Uncle John, a farmer, meant that they could often get ground provisions. Uncle John was the only male in the family and he had received the largest share of the inheritance which was the best and biggest piece of family land. This he used as a farm and he planted yams, potatoes, bananas and had many fruit trees, oranges, mangoes, cherries, and tangerines. Oftentimes mom was sent to him for food and milk. However, they could not take anything from his farm without his permission. If they did, they would be beaten and though it was difficult and tempting, they did without the luscious fruit in order not to irritate their uncle. Fortunately, during mango season, mom and her sisters were able to satisfy their appetite by going for mango walks and returning with their baskets filled with mangoes.

After leaving school, mom thought it necessary to start working so that she could help her mother. One of her earliest ways of earning a living was to assist in the building of roads in her district. Her task was to break the stones and then pile them at a strategic location where they could be collected by the trucks. She enjoyed this very much. As a child one of mom's favourite games was, "go down a Manuel road gal and boy fi go bruk rack stone". After leaving that job, she decided to peddle a variety of produce such as yams, coffee and bananas.

While she was still in the country, mom gave birth to three wonderful girls, Wilhel, who is the oldest, Sonia, the second, and Cutie, the third. Her life became quite difficult so she left the country, for town, in search of a better life.

FROM RURAL TO URBAN

At age 28, mom came to Kingston where she boarded with a small family in Mountain View. They were of Indian descent. Mom stayed with them for awhile and was able to learn a lot from them. Their food and culture were so different and it amazed mom that they even allowed their pet dog to sleep in their bed. At times, mom thought they treated the dog better than her. She eventually moved from there and took a job as a live-in helper at Whitehall.

At that time, the place was bushy and underdeveloped. It was so dark that she had to walk with a lantern at nights. Not only was there no electricity but major roads were not yet constructed and she had to walk through gullies and bushes to get from one point to another.

Shortly after moving, she got baptized at the Clifton New Testament Church of God under the care of Reverend Samuels while setting herself on the pathway to what would eventually become a long and illustrious life.

MOM FINDS HER HUSBAND

One morning at Whitehall, while she was ironing her boss' shirt, she heard the Holy Spirit revealing to her that she was to get married. She immediately shouted, "Hallelujah, thank you Lord." She was unaware that the Lord was speaking to one Lennie Reid, who lived nearby, to go and propose to her. He obeyed. As he made the proposal, she told him that it had been revealed to her that she was to wed but that she did not know who her husband would be. Although mom was dad's senior by eleven years, she was thirty-two years old and he was twenty-one, she accepted his proposal. This direction from the Lord paved the way to an inevitable, successful meeting and friendship with Lennie Reid. This union subsequently gave birth to the Reid family in which five children were produced.

Mom got married to dad on a bright Sunday morning. It was one of the happiest moments of their life. The Clifton Church was filled to capacity. There was such joy and peace on the faces of their guests as they expressed their delight in sharing in such a momentous occasion. They showered them with gifts, so much so that another area had to be created to place the gifts as the designated space was quickly filled. Up to this date, their wedding is said to be one of the biggest that ever took place at Clifton New Testament Church. It was after the wedding that they had their first son, Joseph. Also, mom took her other three children from Manchester and we became one big family. This union between mom and dad lasted over thirty-nine years and ended at the time of her death.

A WARM COMMUNITY

The young couple moved to Manning's Hill Road. They resided in a small, undeveloped community where they leased a piece of land and built a house for themselves. Very few people lived there but the community had an atmosphere of warmth and friendliness as each member was loving and kind. Everyone was their brother's keeper, especially during difficult times.

There was a small shop that served the community. It would be opened as early as seven in the morning and closed as late as ten in the night. This is where mom sent us to shop. Even when the shop was closed she could always send to the shopkeeper. He didn't fuss because he knew his major role was to serve the community at large.

Mom told us that the community was not only bushy but that it also had many graves since the owner of the property had buried his relatives there. Graves were destroyed to create adequate space for the building of new houses. As children, we were warned against playing around the graveside and were told that the ghosts (duppies) would frighten us to death if we interrupted their sleep. This meant little to us and we still enjoyed playing games on the graves.

A WARM COMMUNITY

I can recall one particular night when my brother wrapped himself in a white sheet, made funny sounds and danced in the dark pretending to be a ghost. We screamed for help and mom came rushing out of the room. When she realized that it was our brother she grabbed him, scolded him and warned him never to do that again. It's unfortunate that oral tradition is no longer a dominant part of our culture as nowadays children are no longer told "duppy" stories.

A FAMILY WOMAN AND DISCIPLINARIAN

Mommy demonstrated an unconditional love by being the best mother and wife that she could have ever been. We were all given the time, effort and support needed in our endeavours. With three of her children and husband being blind, she was cautious in remodelling strategies and communication skills as she had to find methods which she could employ to effectively care for us. Mom ensured that her husband's needs were satisfied and that we went to school and were healthy and safe from the dangers of the time. As children, we could not even leave our house without the permission of our parents.

It was fun growing as children together. We played "dolly house" and games of all kinds. Mom would also watch us play our games and laugh. Sometimes she would get involved and play with us. She said she loved to see her children happy. At bedtime, we were told the popular stories of those days such as Anancy stories and "duppy" stories. We were often treated to ice-cream by our mother and she would take us to visit our grandparents in the country. This we enjoyed very much, as it was during these periods that we were able to experience a different lifestyle from the one we were accustomed to in Kingston.

A FAMILY WOMAN AND DISCIPLINARIAN

At an early stage in our lives mom taught us the importance of being clean and responsible. "Cleanliness is next to Godliness" was one of her favourite phrases and so she would give us house work to reinforce this idea. Each person was assigned a specific task so that lessened any need for quarrels about who neglected his responsibility. Some of these duties included washing the dishes, sweeping the yard and cleaning the house.

Although Mommy was a jovial woman, she was also very serious. She used to tell us that the good book, the Holy Bible, said, "You should not save the rod and spoil the child." Being the believer that she was, she punished us whenever we did anything wrong. She would often tell us that it's because she wanted us to "grow good". Whenever we did something wrong we were given extra home work to do or told to find a book and read. If we hurt her feelings and did something that she really didn't like, she would beat – not brutalize – us. At times we would run to dad just to escape the beating but he would hold us and beat us instead. He told us that he must be in agreement with his wife.

I can remember once when we were playing "dolly house" around the backyard and we picked the young almond off the tree. That evening when mom came home and saw what we were doing, she beat all of us; none of us could escape it. There was another incident when my younger sister was rude. Mom got the belt, took her outside and started beating her but our dog, Lion, saved her. Lion used his mouth and pulled the belt from my mother's hand unexpectedly. Mom was frightened and she couldn't find anything else to use so my sister eventually got away. Now that we are grown we sit and laugh about these things but we weren't laughing back then.

VALUES AND ATTITUDES

Haralambos et al, defines values as a belief that is something good and desirable. It defines what is important, worthwhile and worth striving for.

Similarly, norms are said to be a specific guide to action which defines acceptable and appropriate behaviour in a particular situation. Norms are enforced by positive and negative sanctions, that is, rewards and punishments. Sanctions can be informal, such as an approving or disapproving glance, or formal, such as a reward or a fine given by an official body.

Christian values, social values, family values and moral values were what mom instilled in her children. To value yourself, others and property, we were told, were the things that made you a person. She would always tell us that common courtesy like please, sorry, thank you and good morning should always be practised. We were taught to adopt and pass on ethical principles such as love, honesty, kindness, respect, and there was no excuse for ever disrespecting an elder. The proverb 'manners will take you to the four corners of the earth' rang true for my mother as she constantly reverberated this thought.

Our parents educated us about the facts of life. They would constantly say, "Sex is not for children but for responsible adults, and it is a gift given to man by God."

VALUES AND ATTITUDES

Dad also told us that sex comes after marriage and that after every action there are consequences.

We were admonished to always be careful about the way in which we presented ourselves, not only in attire but also in our behaviour, as she strongly believed that a bad attitude towards people could prevent us from accomplishing our goals. Mother also warned us to be careful of the friends we kept. "Show me your company and I tell you who you are" and since "Satan find work for idle hands," it only follows that we were encouraged to keep friends who served as a positive influence.

A SKILFUL AND TALENTED WOMAN

Mom always tried to be an independent lady and so she became an expert at "tun yuh han mek fashion" when things got desperate. She would take syrup and make suck-suck, use coconuts to make coconut drops and when coconuts weren't available, she used peanuts instead. Potato and cornmeal puddings were also sold and it was a delight to us as we could smell the sweet delicious aroma from just about anywhere in the community, which caused our mouths to salivate. She even sold ice to the community members.

My mother's skill wasn't limited to baking as she was skilful in embroidering and crocheting. We would often sit and watch her make beautifully decorated items of various colours and hats which she sold to her church members. She made patchwork sheets for our beds and pillows, used old pieces of cloth to make beautiful rags for the floor, and made pom-poms for girls to wear especially on sports day. She even made curtains during Christmas and because of the skills that she possessed, our house was the most beautifully decorated one in the community during Christmas.

Dancing and singing were also among mom's talent. During her childhood, she loved and enjoyed singing, dancing and acting.

A SKILFUL AND TALENTED WOMAN

While in the country, persons usually called on her to dance because they thought she was a spectacle. Some of the dances she performed were Mash Potato, May Pole, Quadrille and Kumina. However, when she came to town, accepted the Lord and got baptized, she started singing and dancing similar to how David danced and sang. She was then known for her sanctimonious dancing and her playing of the tambourine. Whenever she felt God's presence in the music, her heart, body and soul was propelled to move and allow the Holy Spirit to direct her path.

In addition to these skills, mommy received the spiritual gift of discernment. She could see things before it happened, especially to her children. When mom warned us and we disobeyed, she would say, "I tell you, you cannot say I never warned you. Who cannot hear must feel." She always said she didn't want to be like the man in the Bible who buried his one talent and this she didn't do. She would often go on the streets and witness to persons telling them about God's saving grace. "All praises should go to God who is the Almighty."

MOM OVERCOMES THE ODDS

One serious problem that confronted my mother was when three of her children began to lose their sight: my brother, my sister and I. My sister was the first to experience this. She was hit in her eye, which caused severe pain. Mom had to be in and out of the hospital because my sister was admitted and although an operation was performed, there was nothing the doctors could do to save her sight. She was fourteen years old. Unfortunately, my brother and I had the same experience which meant that my mother now had to care for three visually impaired children. She spent endless nights in the hospital with us and she never once became bitter as she realized and often said, "This is my cross so I must bear it."

Another challenge that faced her was when my younger brother, at age two, pulled down a bowl of hot cornmeal porridge on himself. His belly was severely burnt. She rushed him to the children's hospital where he was admitted, treated and discharged.

Whenever problems confronted my mother, she cried in order to release the heartache and tension. But, with her God by her side and encouragement from friends and relatives, she always overcame the odds.

MOM, A COMMUNITY WOMAN

Mom lived in the community for 35 years. She loved it dearly. She made sure that her community was clean and properly looked after. It was through my mother's efforts that the community got a stand pipe that served the neighbourhood. We also had electric light. Whatever was happening in the community, positive or negative, the first person the residents would call on was 'Sister Reid.' She made herself available at all times to attend to the needs of the people. She was known for her faithfulness, humility, kindness and love. In the 1970's, the community's infrastructure and population developed rapidly as houses were built by children and grandchildren who sought to establish themselves in the area.

Sometimes mom would visit the elderly in the neighbourhood and share a bowl of soup with them for which they were always grateful. She would sit at their doorsteps and chat, or alternatively, they would visit her at home. Whenever this happened we would puff up our faces because we could not get her attention, no matter how we cried. She would usually say to us "You don't see mi talking, have some manners and wait." They talked for lengthy hours.

MEMORIES OF MY JAMAICAN MOTHER

On the 12th of September, 1988, Gilbert struck Jamaica. We took it for a joke when we heard that a storm was coming. Mom and dad were serious because they had already experienced hurricane Charlie. We listened to them and battened up, preparing with anxiety waiting to see what the experience would be like. The day began with a cloudless sky and brilliant sunshine with no indication that a storm was eminent. When it came, it hit us very hard. It was a lovely sight to see at first, before roofs were being blown off, houses were flooded out and furniture was damaged. When the wind became fierce and rain started to pour heavily we stopped our laughing, the excitement died and we started to cry fearing that our house would be destroyed. Our parents called us all in a room which they knew was safe and told us to calm down. Mommy told us to pray that the storm would pass us by and that our house would stand firm. And it did. Persons who were affected by the hurricane took refuge in the church.

After the storm passed we really gave thanks to God for allowing us to escape the damages of the hurricane. Mom went outside and walked around in the community to see what assistance she could render. She removed fallen trees that were blocking the pathway and shared whatever food and water she had with those who had none. She tried to bring cheer to the victims of the hurricane and spoke to the persons in authority, members of parliament and pastors, who could assist in the redevelopment of the community.

Mom and Dad's 35th Wedding Anniversary

Mom and her grandson, Shevaun

Mom playing the piano

A HELPFUL AND INDUSTRIOUS MOM

Though mom was hard working, she was a helpful woman who would go beyond the call of duty to assist anyone. One evening as mom came in tired from work she heard that a little boy fell out of a mango tree and broke his hand. She rushed to the scene where she saw him yelling and wailing in pain. Those who had gathered around him asked, "Whose child is this?" but mommy took him in her arms, stopped a taxi and rushed with him to the hospital.

Another instance in which mom demonstrated her helpful nature happened while she was on her veranda relaxing and someone called, "Sister Reid, Sister Reid help!" As she dashed off the veranda she was in time to see a woman take the hot boiling water off the fire and throw it on her boyfriend. He had dark complexion and his skin became white instantly. Mommy attended to him and so he recovered nicely. Surprisingly, until this day the same couple is still living together and their relationship is now sound.

One late night mom was fast asleep and dad heard a knocking on the gate. Mom woke up and discovered that it was a young lady with her two children with nowhere to sleep. Immediately mom called her in and found space in the house for her. That lady is now married and has her own house. Her children are now professionals. Mommy encouraged the young people in the neighbourhood to find something worthwhile to do with their lives. She would even make contact with persons who she knew was able to assist them. Mom would go the extra mile to help anyone. She gave one young lady a head start in life. That lady now has her own business which is a grocery shop. To this end, people can testify of the help they received from my mother.

Mom's entire life was built and fashioned on helping people from every walk of life. This she did with little or no fuss even when those in need demonstrated undesirable behaviour and discouraged her from helping. She would respond by saying, "This is my calling and my reward is sure in heaven." Her favourite hymn she always hummed when she thought about giving assistance to others is:

"Little is much when God is in it. Labour not for wealth or fame. There is a crown and you can win it, if you go in Jesus name. When our conflict here is ended and our work on earth is done, He will say if you are faithful, welcome home my child well done."

Being able to provide for her family was a priority for mom and so she always had a job. She worked at the Shortwood Teacher's College as a chef from the early 1960s to 1973. She then moved on to another job as an office attendant at the Manning's Hill Road Medical Center where she worked until retirement. At that time Manning's Hill Road was bushy so her dog, Lion, walked with her in the wee hours of the morning all the way to the door of the Shortwood Teacher's College. Lion would be back in the afternoon for the return journey. One day he was hit by a car and died, and of course mom cried when she heard the news.

While at the Manning's Hill Road Medical Center my mother worked under many titles. She was an office attendant who also periodically manned the telephone. She always answered by saying, "Manning's Hill Road Medical Center, pleasant morning." People who called the center said they felt welcomed when they heard the sweet, chirpy tone of her voice ringing in their ears. She attended to the patients as well. She talked with them, offered comfort and gave them a sense of hope. One patient said that talking to her, although ill, he felt better. Mom also worked as a nurse. She attended to patients and dressed cuts until they could be seen by a doctor. Dr. Betton, who was a medical doctor and her employer, described mom as a courteous, industrious and well rounded worker who could fit in any capacity. She never frowned nor fussed when asked to do anything, even to go on the road to deliver mails or to purchase his lunch.

MOM, A POWERFUL AND STRONG BLACK WOMAN

Mom was a fervent Christian woman, saved, sanctified and filled with the Holy Spirit's divine power for service. Anything she did she tried to do it under the anointing of the Holy Spirit, being led by him. I remember in 1979, when I was nine years old that my brother, my sister and I had Mumps, a contagious disease that affects children. That morning our parents left for work leaving us under the supervision of our neighbour. She came by every now and then to see how we were doing and what we were doing. We were all there in the house in pain when suddenly we heard a voice shouting, "Fire! Fire!" Everyone started running towards the voice with buckets of water on their heads and in their hands. I did not remember anything about the pain, I just ran for my nephew who was one year of age, picked him up in my arms and dashed out of the house calling for my bother and sister. It was a Kerosene oil stove that blew up, catching the house on fire.

When mom heard that the whole neighbourhood was on fire she came running asking for her children. The houses were very close to each other and because of the fruit trees hanging over them the fire spread rapidly. Mommy went and stood before the fire, pointed to it and spoke to it under the anointing. I saw when the fire dashed back with full force before catching our house. The firemen came just in time to put out the fire. Everyone marvelled at this strange sight and could not believe what they had seen. Their comments were, "Sister is a powerful woman, look what she has done." But one thing that I missed, loved and valued dearly was a golden spoon that mom gave to me as a birthday gift. I lost it in the fire heap. I cherished it so much.

Mommy was a strong and beautiful, black, Jamaican woman. She was charming, loving and full of dignity and integrity. Her character portrayed someone who everyone wanted to emulate. She was strong physically and spiritually. Her faith was what made her strong and she lived a healthy lifestyle, along with her husband standing beside her, strengthening her. She could move mountains. "One can chase a thousand, while two put ten thousand to flight." I remember that one night when I was a child, I took ill so badly that mom rushed me to the hospital. The doctor could not tell what was wrong with me. Mommy and daddy bonded their faith together, laid their hands on me and prayed under the anointing. After receiving the prayer I got better. "A family that prays and plays together stays together." It was a good feeling having both parents together, who we had a fulfilling relationship with, knowing that we could call on them at any time.

MOM WATCHES HER CHILDREN EXCEL

Despite the odds, mommy and daddy wanted to see us excel and reach our full potential in life. We could not allow anyone to hinder us from trying. They went on to say "We should aim for excellence, strive for higher heights and reach for the stars." They implored us to work to the best of our abilities whatever we put our minds and hands to. We were advised that when trying we will come upon obstacles but we must overcome them and move on in life.

While we were attending school, mom and dad visited our schools to see how well we were performing in our school work. When doing well they praised us and said, "Keep up the good work and continue to do well." If not, they would scold us and encourage us to try harder. They would also take our reports from our teachers and look at them. Mom would see to it that we did less playing and attended to our homework. At times there was no television for us to watch as it would distract us from focusing on our lessons. Mom told us, "If you know your head cannot take the studying try and learn a skill." She never appreciated laziness.

After leaving school, some of us went on to further studies. Our parents did not have the money to help us so we worked and helped further ourselves. My sister and I went on to university

MOM WATCHES HER CHILDREN EXCEL

while one brother went to college and the others are self-employed. Mommy and daddy lived to see their children pass the worst and their words did not fall on deaf ears.

A GOD FEARING AND DEVOTED MOM

Mommy was a God fearing and devoted Christian woman. She loved the Lord. She raised us in the fear and knowledge of God. Every morning at five she would wake us up to have early morning devotion and in the evenings, both mom and dad would have prayer meeting. Sometimes we frowned because we did not want to come out of our warm and cozy beds but we could not help but to get up. For our parents, we must go to church. We were sent to Vacation Bible School during the summer.

At Christmas, she would dress us in our best Sunday wear and send us to Christmas parties, treats and concerts. As children we believed in Santa Claus. On Christmas morning, we normally awoke to see gifts on our beds, believing that it was Santa who had put it there. Easter time was mom's favourite holiday because it was not commercialized. It was holy, peaceful and sanctimonious. On Good Friday, mommy would avoid cooking any meat with blood including chicken, beef, pork and mutton. So, very often, she ended up not cooking on Good Friday. We were taught about God at home, at church and at school. As a result of that we all accepted the Lord and are living holy Christian lives.

A DEVOUT CHRISTIAN

Mommy gave full service to the church for over forty three years, working in different areas. She worked as Sergeant at Arms in the Sunday school department, group leader for the family training hour and the lady's ministry. She was involved in a singing group for many years before being a founding member of the lady's choir. Mommy also sang on the National Combined Choir. Sometimes she would work in the tuck shop on Sunday mornings, selling grater cakes and other pastries to the children. She also worked as an usherette, welcoming visitors to the church. One visitor said of my mother, "Sister makes me feel so welcome." As a result of working in the church for many years, mom was awarded the family training hour crown. I once heard my mom singing aloud in the bathroom a couple lines of a song that embodies her beliefs:

"*May the life I live speak for me. May the work I have done speak for me. While I am resting in my grave, there is nothing I can say. So may the life I live speak for me.*"

Mommy was well known for going to rallies, conventions and funerals. She was also devoted to her choir practice and other activities of the church. It was an aspiration for mommy to be a musician for the church. She started piano lessons and went on as far as grade two. Unfortunately, her dream was not accomplished.

RETIREMENT

The time came for mom to retire from Manning's Hill Road Medical Center. It was a tough decision for her to accept but she had no other choice. She was offered a trip overseas by my sister but mom declined stating that she would not leave Jamaica and her family even for a day. We believed that it was time for her to come home and rest herself. "The heart is willing but the flesh is weak." After mom retired she bought a piano which she played in order to occupy her mind. She also decided to give her service full time to the church. When it was time for rally, she enjoyed herself very much. She would knock her tambourine, shaking it high in the air, running and dancing, singing, "A rally time, a rally time. Oh! Oh! A rally time!" For convention, it did not matter where it was held she would always be in attendance. Funerals were no exception. Anywhere the funeral was being held she would call her friend "Willy! Yuh ready?" So they would both go. They did not care where it was.

MOM REFLECTS

Sometimes mommy would sit and reflect, looking back from whence she was coming, to where she had reached in life. She watched the time move from one era to the next. She was amazed at how technology had made popular some of the things she accepted and some of the things she rejected. She expressed surprise when she saw me on my computer doing my school work. Her comments were, "Technology has made life much easier for young people. In my time I was not so privileged. When I was growing up we did not have any television to watch and now I can sit and relax and watch my own TV and even cable." One thing for sure that mommy rejected was the fact that people wore cheerful colours to funerals. She believed that it should be black and white as these colours represented the sombre mood that the death of a loved one would bring.

Mommy would knock board when she saw her children excel. She said that she felt pleased and proud of us because we did not bring any shame and disgrace on the family. "People who discouraged me telling to runaway leave unno, me only sorry seh some a dem nuh deh round to see unno." During her reflection she would laugh or show disgust, based on the memory.

ILLNESS, HOSPITALIZATION AND DEATH

At the age of fifty, mommy was diagnosed with diabetes. Diabetes is one of the chronic diseases that affect most elderly people. As the disease started to take a hold of her body she began to visit the doctor regularly. She became sickly and complained about aches and pain all over her body. She was instructed by the doctor to take her medication, do her exercises, and follow her diet restrictions and rest.

Her immediate family, relatives, friends and church brethren began to rally around her as they noticed her illness becoming worse. One night mommy took sick badly. We rushed her to the hospital where she was admitted. When I visited the hospital, she was not responding to me and tears filled my eyes because I could not see her although she was looking at me, which I did not know. I went to the doctor who was sitting near by and began talking to her about my mother. She told me that she was okay, and that she was recovering well but some persons doubted this. One day while walking in the community, someone said to me, "Your mother look like she naa go mek it so you can start plan her funeral." My reply was, "Mommy soon come home and dance in church let all of us see." Everyone lost hope including my brothers and sisters. I was the only one who was hopeful. Eventually mommy was discharged from the hospital. She recovered so well that she even danced in church. The same person who gave up on my mother came to me and said, "I saw Sister Reid dancing in church, you really have faith." We all felt good that mom was better.

It was after a year that mom took ill again. One late Wednesday night I stayed in my room and heard mommy groaning. I jumped up, rushed into her room and softly knocked on the door. It was open, and my daddy and I went in and found mom in terrible pain. She was taken to the hospital and admitted. Early Saturday morning someone called the house and gave us the news that she had died.

Upon her death, the family went through the process of grieving as recognized by Dr. Elizabeth Kubler-Ross. These five responses to grief are:

Shock and Numbness: Even though death was expected, the reality of it came as a great shock. Death may not seem real and denial can be a chosen part to protect against the pain.

Guilt: People may feel a sense of failure after someone dies. Others will feel guilty out of proportion to their responsibility, or will feel guilty when it is not appropriate.

Anger: Anger is a common and normal reaction to death, and is usually directed at the person who has died. However, since it is very difficult to be angry at the person who has died, this gets displaced at other persons or things. It needs to be expressed otherwise it will turn inwards and cause depression and physical problems.

ILLNESS, HOSPITALIZATION AND DEATH

Depression: A time of great sadness and loneliness that comes with the death of a friend or loved one. It is a difficult time and one that needs to be experienced. Grieving takes time; don't rush the process.

Resolution: It is the process of accepting our loss and integrating that loss into our heads so we can remember our loved ones with joy rather than deep pain. Once we have resolved our grief we can move on to develop relationships with others.

Mommy had lived a fulfilling life before God and persons who knew her could testify to that fact. She had a grand and well-planned funeral. The church was full to capacity as persons from all walks of life attended. Mom is survived by her husband, eight children, fourteen grandchildren, three great grand children, three sisters, one uncle who is now one hundred and three years old, and a host of other relatives and friends.

"May the life I live speak for me, May the work that I have done speak for me, When I am resting in my grave, There is nothing I can say, So may the life I live speak for me."

Mommy made her transition from this life on the 29th of January 2005. She was laid to rest at Dovecot Memorial Gardens.

"Goodbye to pain and woe, Hello to a brand new home. Goodbye to sin and strife, Hello to a brand new life. Goodbye all the sinners, Christians never die. So we know mommy only said goodbye."

TRIBUTE # 1: HER THREE SISTERS, ESTELLA, ICILYN, & YVONNE & UNCLE JOHN, WHO IS NOW 103 YEARS OLD.

Phyliss was one of the best sisters we ever had. She was loving, caring and kind. As an adolescent, her charismatic personality made her an attractive and charming sister. She was always assisting our mother with us and other citizens in the district by delivering meals prepared by our mother. Our sister was the one who paved the way for us. She was the first one to launch out. When she left for town she sent for us and took us under her wings. She allowed us to live near to her. Therefore we thank her for keeping the family unified and in harmony. "United we stand, divided we fall." She would go the extra mile to see that we were at ease. Because of what she had done we will always remember our dearest sister, Phyliss.

TRIBUTE # 2: HER HUSBAND, LENNIE REID

The lover of my life, Phyliss Blake Reid, she was my wife. A virtuous woman I surely found, she just knew how to take care of her man all the time. She cooked my food and ensured that my clothes were clean. She bore all my children, in that I am pleased. She was faithful, honest, loving and kind, sweet memories that will never depart from my mind. I'll never regret taking that woman for my wife; we lived harmoniously until the day she died.

TRIBUTE # 3: Shopkeeper & Mentor, Mother Ivy Don.

Sister Reid was one of my most faithful customers. It was at my store that she did all her shopping. If she could not get what she wanted at my grocery store then she would eventually go somewhere else. Some items that she purchased included bread, milk, sugar, bun and other household items. Sister Reid was not only my customer but she was a good friend to me. "A good friend is better than pocket money." At times she would come to me, telling me her problems. I would try to help her in finding solutions for them.

We both attended the same church. She helped in building up the structure of the church as she carried the cement mixture that was mixed by the working men. She was a hardworking woman who never said no when asked to do anything. She was the type of person who I could trust and depend on to do anything for me. Therefore my shop was always opened to welcome her at any time of the day. Even if she did not have the money she still got what she wanted for herself and her family.

Sister Reid once told me that she saw me as her role model, someone she could look up to and someone who had really influenced her life. Whenever she passed by my shop door she would always call out, "Don! Don! Oh Mother Don!" I will always remember Sister Reid for the kindness and love that she gave. It feels good to know that I really motivated her and she was grateful for that. May her soul rest in peace.

TRIBUTE # 4: Her Eight Children

Mommy, the best mother in the world. She loved, nurtured, and supported us. Our gratitude, love, respect and thanks we gave her for being such a warm and caring mother to us. She treated us well so we toiled to make her proud. In our hearts we will never forget our mom. She was our favourite person. Humble, hardworking and helpful she was, she never got weary of us calling on her. "Mommy!" She knew that we put our trust in her. For mom, the only places of interest for her children were from home to school to church and back home but she ensured that we were socialized with others. These are great landmarks which will never depart from us but we will pass them on to our children. We thank God for giving us mom. She played her role and she played it well. Mama we want you to know, loving you was like food to our souls.

TRIBULTE # 5: Nieces & Nephews

Phyliss was the best aunt we ever had. She was loving, caring, gentle and kind. She assisted our parents during times of difficulty. She accommodated us in her home. Because of this her children and us grew up as brothers and sisters. Aunty gave us food, clothing and she shared her warm sentiments with us. Whenever she did not see any of us she would worry. She treated us as if we were her own.

Whenever we asked for something the only time we never received it was when she never had it. She gave us money, she would buy us sweets and at Christmas time we would receive our gifts. Even as adults she would assist us in decision-making because what looked right in our eyes, to her seemed wrong. She would call us aside and talk to us about life, putting us on the right path.

Aunty will always be remembered for her good deeds on earth and the love that she had shown us. May her soul rest in peace.

TRIBUTE # 6: Neighbour, Victoria Ratrick

I knew Reidy from back in the 70's, the minute I came to the community to live. We both shared anything we had with each other. She gave me dinner, I gave her dinner. This was how we lived as neighbours. Sometimes I would leave my children in her care for her to supervise them until I returned. She could do the same with me. Reidy was a peaceful woman. She was never in conflict with anyone. At times I would go over to her house, sit on her door step and laugh and talk with her. We would even break the word of God with each other. We sang 'sankys' and songs from the hymnals. I loved Reidy because there was never a dull moment around her. I will always remember her, especially the times we spent together.

TRIBUTE # 7: Former Employer, Dr. Audley H. Betton

Phyliss Reid was introduced to me in 1975 by Dr. Valerie Brown. I was immediately warmed by her remarkable strength beneath that soft, seemingly simple personality. She was someone whose ability to overcome challenges had won the admiration of all who knew her. With a husband and three of her children being visually impaired, she was caring and supportive to them and everyone around her in a manner that was unique.

It was no surprise to anyone that she was invited to work with us as we sought to offer health care to the Manning's Hill Road Community. She would always go beyond the call of duty to offer a word of cheer and comfort to ailing patients. Her words of advice and encouragement often took precedence over her work.

She made it a point of her duty to understand and organize all procedures in the day to day running of the office, and would seek to train new members of staff, regardless of their portfolio. She was the first to offer assistance in an emergency, assisting in suturing, dressing and assessing patients. Answering the phone came naturally, and she adopted the title of "Nurse" after assisting in a delivery one morning when she was the only assistant at work.

She was our 'eyes and ears' in the community, and ran her own dressing clinic early in the morning for the underprivileged – something I doubt she knew we were aware of. Given the chance, she would have provided tea, coffee and snacks for every patient who needed it.

I saw an unusual side of her caring and emotional strength when her mother died. She showed the same interest to every member of her family whenever they had to visit the doctor, placing their care in the hands of the Lord.

It was, however, her strong will to survive and live Christian principles that I am sure endeared her to many. With meagre resources, she raised her eight children, encouraging them to excel against all odds. The success they are today is undoubtedly the result of the resilience instilled in them by her example. Nothing stopped her from achieving her goals.

In her latter years, she struggled with diabetes, hypertension and heart failure that would have easily overcome the faint hearted. In and out of the hospital, weekly visits to the doctor assisted by her children and grandchildren and a host of tablets to be taken daily, her spirit never wavered.

The legacy she has left behind, I have no doubt, will inspire her family as they continue to win the admiration of the wider community. The example she has set and the principles she stood for, will never be forgotten by the many persons whose lives she touched, as a humble, caring, strong and devoted mother, grandmother, wife, adopted mother, role model and Christian woman.

TRIBUTE # 8: Neighbour, Minna McLeod

Mrs. Reid was a good woman to me. When I was unemployed and could not get a job nor think of anything to do, she called me aside and said to me, "Minna, you can do a little selling." I told her that I didn't know what to sell and she told me to sell some fruits. She gave me a push start in my business and I am still benefiting from it. I always visited her making sure she got her fruits because I knew that she loved fruits. Mrs. Reid would sometimes come to my gate and call out, "Minna! Minna!" When I heard her I would dash out with fruits in my hands.

She was a pleasant woman, always smiling no matter what the problem was. She had a lively spirit. If you were feeling down hearted while talking to her, she would cheer you up. I will never forget the many things she did for me. Her personality really impacted me and so I will always remember her kindness and how wonderful she was to me.

TRIBUTE # 9: Hyacinth Williams & Family

God has conferred on womanhood,
A true nobility.
And she who gladly fills that role,
Can shape man's destiny
No man is poor who has had a godly mother.

This statement above highlights the characteristics of Phyliss Reid: mother, wife, grandmother, confidante and friend. To many persons, Phyliss Reid may have seemed like an ordinary person but to her 'August family' she represented a woman of undeniable and incomparable love. A phenomenal woman, her strong faith and sacrificial love have ensured her family's self worth, maximum accomplishment, upward mobility and a deep sense of their heritage.

For Mrs. Reid, the sky was the limit for her family. Being multi-skilled, she made sure that each member of the family was economically stable. Her life reflected all the characteristics of the "virtuous woman" in Proverbs 31: 10-31. Not only did she maintain a long and lasting relationship with her God and her husband, but she also established the basic principles of a Godly heritage which were instilled in the lives of her children. To her household, she was similar to King Solomon's virtuous woman: housewife, merchant, trader, agriculturist, giver, fashion designer, teacher, family protector, royalty, and a queen among women. Without a doubt, Mrs. Reid has left her family a heritage which will never decay.

Today, though dead, the memory of Mrs. Reid lives on. Her family and the wider community are proud of her accomplishments in providing for them parental and Christian guidance. Truly, her parenting skills were not only in words but were demonstrated, thus ensuring academic, interpersonal and socio-economic achievements for her children. Although visually challenged, Doreen, Jackie and Joseph have become scholars. They have ascended the 'ladder' of academic achievements and bravely excelled where sighted persons dare to trod. These children are living examples of how positive parenting can influence the development of individuals.

While Doreen's book "The Life of a True Father" represents a glorious tribute to her dad, the follow up to her mother is a fitting tribute to a woman who has been the 'bedrock' of her household. Not only was she the torch that lit the flame of faith, perseverance and success, but despite various hardships, she provided an environment that encouraged and influenced the positive development of her family, friends and general society.

The life, work and worth of Mrs. Reid will continue to speak clearly. She is not dead; she has only made her transition from earth's physical environment to her spiritual home. Instead of living in earth's shadows, she has taken the journey to heaven's realm, where her security, comfort and everlasting joy is guaranteed in the presence of her resurrected Lord. May her soul enjoy the blessedness of Heaven's joy. "Blessed are those who die in the Lord from now on. They are blessed indeed, for they will rest from all their toils and trials, and their good deeds will follow me." (Revelations 14:14)

To the Reid family we say congratulations, may your resilience, family commitments and achievements serve as beacons of inspiration to others. We give thanks to God for mothers who not only care for their children physically but also nurture them spiritually. Mothers like those are truly unforgettable.

TRIBUTE # 10: HER VISUALLY IMPAIRED CHILDREN: JOSEPH, JACQUELINE AND DOREEN

To us, our mom is the best mother in the entire world. She loved, cared for us and treated us well. Each of her children was treated equally and none was placed higher than the other. We were all given impartial amounts of love, support and nurturing. She was not overprotective nor was she fearful of her children going out alone. She would always pray on our way out and upon our safe arrival back home her usual quotation was, "Thank Jesus for allowing you to reach back home safely."

In spite of the disabilities faced by us, her children, we were not deterred from achieving our dreams. Mom taught us how to become independent as we learnt to cook, clean, wash and take proper care of our bodies. She realized that the public was always looking at us whenever we went out and so we were taught to groom ourselves properly although we could not see. She encouraged us to strive for excellence and not to limit ourselves to any disabilities. Jackie and I went to the University of the West Indies where we did our B.A. in Social Work, and Joseph went to Jamaica School of Music where he was trained as a musician. Mom was always proud of us while she watched us excel.

Mom, we thank you for living an exemplary life that we all could be pleased with. Truly we greatly appreciate it and your life will continually be a landmark in our lives because indeed you are a God-sent mother.

TRIBUTE # 11: Mr. & Mrs. Trowers

Sister Reid was a blessed woman. She had helped us in so many situations. There was never a dull moment around her. One thing that stands out the most in my mind is seeing her at church, dancing, singing, shouting and playing her tambourine. She never got weary of praising her God.

She was a family woman, always taking care of her husband and children. Regardless of their disabilities, she made time for them and ensured that they were always fine. Although she did not have much to give her family financially, she was not a bother to anyone. Sister Reid put her trust in God to provide for her and her family and He did.

Whenever she was in need she would pray to God and He would provide in a miraculous way. I can remember that one day she testified in church that she did not have any food or money in the house and she prayed to the Lord. God sent a church sister to her with food and money and she really gave God thanks.

I always heard her say, "God does not give you more than you can bear". I could tell you many more stories about this wonderful woman but time and space would not allow. May her soul rest in perfect peace.

TRIBUTE # 12: Church Sister, Lorna Cranston

Sister Reid accepted the Lord in her life during the ministry of Rev. Samuel while he was pastor of Clifton New Testament Church many years ago. Not contented with just getting saved, she soon found work to do in her Master's vineyard. She started in the Family Training Hour (FTH) where her work earned her many awards.

Her love for children placed her in the Sunday school as a Sergeant of Arms. This duty meant that she had to be at church by 8:30 each Sunday morning to meet the children at the gate and guide them to their classes. Rain or shine, she could be seen at her post every Sunday morning. She did not know how to say no to church duties so she accepted every one that was given to her. She loved to sing and so she became a foundation member of the Women's Choir and she never missed the National Convention Choir each year.

Sister Reid never allowed her church duties to get between her family and her so every Sunday morning, after attending to all her Sunday school children, she could be seen coming across the street with Doreen and Jackie as she brought them to church. Her love of people was not just in her home but in her community as she readily opened her door to all who were in need and helped in whatever way she could. I turned to her when I needed someone to help collect items from the Poor Relief Office for the shut-ins. She smiled at me with her pretty pink gum and said "Yes". She would go to Half-Way-Tree every Thursday morning and stand in a long line in the sun and wait for each name to be called. She took nothing in return for her time but would always say, "We have to help wi one another cause we are all one".

Sister Reid has run her race, her work is done and she will now receive her crown of life. To her family, she has lived a life that you can follow because she lived and loved and served her God. As she gives up this house of clay, she can now say:

I have finished with this house of clay,
Please kindly and gently lay it away;
And let me rest from this life of pain.
I have started to do my Master's work,
Never a duty did I shirk.
I am tired now so let me rest
So, tenderly, carefully lay it away.

TRIBUTE # 13: Grandson, Shevaun Booth

I loved my grandma because she loved me. Whenever I wanted to watch the television, the answer was always yes. The only time she said no was when something went wrong, for example, when there was a hurricane or when there was lightning.

Whenever I wanted money she would always go into her purse and take it out and give it to me. I used it to buy sweets, cheese trix and bag juice.

I remember the time when I went overseas to my mother, and when I came back to Jamaica, she was so happy to see me; she welcomed me with a kiss and a big hug. Sometimes grandma would look at me and laugh. I just loved to be around her. She was so loving, caring and kind.

Grandma, I will always remember you when I am feeling sad and blue. Some silly jokes that we laughed at whenever I remember them they always make my day. Once again I say, "I love you".

TRIBUTE # 14: Family Friend, Anthony Lawrence

Mrs. Reid was known to me for the past thirty five years. When she got married my sister was a flower girl. She was a wonderful woman of God and a close friend of the family. She was thoughtful and sympathetic to whosoever she came across in her lifetime, both children and adults.

TRIBUTE

She wasn't a rich person but she was content with whatsoever she had. She was never a beggar while growing her children. Before she begged, she would give her children porridge three times a day.

She loved God and her church. You would never be tired to be around her. She is sadly missed by everyone. I hope to see her again because I know she is in heaven.

LESSONS LEARNED

The core values of life, our mum ensured were instilled in us as children. These values are:

a. **Personal Values**: One of the most important personal value that we learnt was the need to love and accept ourselves. It was only after this that we could love others. Mom taught us that personal values are the things that are dear to us such as money, house, food and clothing. From a very early age we were taught the importance and value of money but we were always reminded that although it was valuable and we needed to save; 'the love of money is the root of all evil'. For other personal values we learnt how to care for them in order for them to be useful for long periods.

b. **Family Values**: Families are the foundation of every society and we felt that our family, with mum at its head, played an integral part in building our community. As a family we were always united no matter what differences occurred and this is what we continue to practise daily.

c. **Moral Values**: It was impossible to have a mother like her and not have strong beliefs and principles. First and most important we learned to believe in God, to worship Him, to pray and to read our Bibles, even a chapter, each day. Of course, we had to obey the Ten Commandments that were laid down by our Lord. She taught us to respect the opinion of others and not to impose our beliefs on others, and were warned against discriminating against others for whatever reason, race, class or creed.

d. Societal Values: All of these values helped us in being better citizens of Jamaica. This was because we learned to love and respect our country. Therefore, obeying the laws of the land and exercising our right to vote were duties we had to practise.

These principles mom used as guidelines to direct our lives, even in adulthood.

www.ingramcontent.com/pod-product-compliance
Lightning Source LLC
Chambersburg PA
CBHW031308060426
42444CB00032B/692